LAZY
CAKE
COOKIES
& MORE

LAZY
CAKE
COOKIES
& MORE

DELICIOUS, SHORTCUT DESSERTS
WITH 5 INGREDIENTS OR LESS

JENNIFER PALMER

Page 8: © Dean Mitchell/iStockphoto.com; 11: © milarka/iStockphoto.com; 13: © Brent Hofacker/Shutterstock.com; 14, 15: © Perspectives – Jeff Smith/Shutterstock.com; 16: © Anna Kurzaeva/iStockphoto.com; 18: © Viktar/iStockphoto.com; 19: © Lauri Patterson/iStockphoto.com; 20: © huePhotography/iStockphoto.com; 23: © burwellphotography/iStockphoto.com; 24: © Miguel Garcia Saavedra/Shutterstock.com; 25: © Intellistudies/iStockphoto.com; 26: © Stieglitz/iStockphoto.com; 29: © agcreations/iStockphoto.com; 30, 33: © TheCrimsonMonkey/iStockphoto.com; 34, 35: © Alice Tsygankova/Shutterstock.com; 36: © Southern Light Studios/Shutterstock.com; 38: © Igors Ruskavos/Shutterstock.com; 39: © TSchon/iStockphoto.com; 40: © El Nariz/Shutterstock.com; 42: © Evikka/Shutterstock.com; 45: © A_Lein/Shutterstock.com; 46: © AnjelikaGr/Shutterstock.com; 47: © Olaf Speier/Shutterstock.com; 49: © MaraZe/Shutterstock.com; 51, 114: © matka_Wariatka/Shutterstock.com; 53: © Evgeny Karandaev/Shutterstock.com; 55: © dsmoulton/iStockphoto.com; 59: © Sarah Bossert/iStockphoto.com; 60, 61: © JMichl/iStockphoto.com; 62: © Zigzag Mountain Art/Shutterstock.com; 64: © zoryanchik/Shutterstock.com; 66: © Texturis/Shutterstock.com; 67: © Elena Shashkina/Shutterstock.com; 68: © Innershadows Photography/Shutterstock.com; 71: © vm2002/Shutterstock.com; 72: © Charles Place/Shutterstock.com; 75: © Dionisvera/Shutterstock.com; 77: © letterberry/iStockphoto.com; 79: © IngridHS/iStockphoto.com; 80: © Agnes Kantaruk/Shutterstock.com; 83: © Dream79/Shutterstock.com; 84: © Tomikmalish/iStockphoto.com; 85: © BW Folsom/Shutterstock.com; 86, 87: © Shaiith/iStockphoto.com; 88: © fcafotodigital/iStockphoto.com; 92: © Shebeko/Shutterstock.com; 94: © Guzel Studio/Shutterstock.com; 95: © mythja/Shutterstock.com; 96: © Tagstock1/Shutterstock.com; 99: © Amallia Eka/Shutterstock.com; 100, 103: © Erika Follansbee/Shutterstock.com; 104, 105: AnastasiaKopa/Shutterstock.com; 106: © Tomophafan/iStockphoto.com; 108: © RTimages/iStockphoto.com; 109: © Stephanie Frey/Shutterstock.com; 110: © Anna Quaglia/iStockphoto.com; 111: © topseller/Shutterstock.com; 112: Nattika/Shutterstock.com; © 113: © mphilips007/iStockphoto.com; 117: © Olha Afanasieva/Shutterstock.com; 118: © StudioThreeDots/iStockphoto.com; 119: © Svetlana Foote/Shutterstock.com; 121: © Miuda/Shutterstock.com; 123: © al1962/Shutterstock.com; 124: © KaraBrennan/iStockphoto.com

Front cover (clockwise from top right): © haha21/iStockphoto.com; © kreinick/iStockphoto.com; © huePhotography/iStockphoto.com; © jatrax/iStockphoto.com; © AlexStar/iStockphoto.com; © subjug/iStockphoto.com
Back cover: © Alexander Sherstobitov/iStockphoto.com; © Southern Light Studios/Shutterstock.com

For information about permission to reproduce selections from this book,
write to Permissions, The Countryman Press,
500 Fifth Avenue, New York, NY 10110

For information about special discounts for bulk purchases,
please contact W. W. Norton Special Sales at
specialsales@wwnorton.com or 800-233-4830.

Library of Congress Cataloging-in-Publication Data

Palmer, Jennifer, 1980- author.
Lazy cake cookies & more : delicious, shortcut desserts with 5 ingredients or less / Jennifer Palmer.
    pages cm
Includes bibliographical references and index.
ISBN 978-1-58157-370-1 (pbk. : alk. paper)
1. Desserts. 2. Quick and easy cooking. I. Title. II. Title: Lazy cake cookies and more.
TX773.P245 2015
641.86--dc23
                        2015028904

The Countryman Press
www.countrymanpress.com

A division of W. W. Norton & Company, Inc.,
500 Fifth Avenue, New York, NY 10110
www.wwnorton.com

ISBN 978-1-58157-370-1 (pbk.)

10 9 8 7 6 5 4 3 2 1

"I THINK BAKING COOKIES IS EQUAL TO
QUEEN VICTORIA RUNNING AN EMPIRE.
THERE'S NO DIFFERENCE IN HOW SERIOUSLY
YOU TAKE THE JOB, HOW SERIOUSLY YOU
APPROACH YOUR WHOLE LIFE."

—MARTHA STEWART

LAZY CAKE COOKIES & MORE
CONTENTS

Introduction: Welcome to Lazy Cake Cookies & More!

If you're like me, baking is one of the most enjoyable activities in your life. It's right up there with sunny days by the pool, late-night dinner parties, and, well, eating what you bake and sharing it with loved ones. Baking is truly a way to relax, recharge, de-stress, and embrace your creative side. So let's get baking!

If "lazy cakes" aren't already a part of your baking routine, I hope these recipes will inspire you to create delicious, easy treats on the regular. They're great for when you're pressed for time, or just feeling lazy! Inside you'll find more than fifty recipes for cookies, pies, cakes, and more—all with just five ingredients or less. That's right, these are delicious concoctions you can make in a flash, without endless measurements of teaspoons and tablespoons. While I love a complex recipe, sometimes it's nice to just grab a box of lemon cake mix, a tub of Cool Whip, and an egg and make a batch of light and sweet Lemon Dream Drop Cookies. Or add peanut butter, condensed milk, and vanilla to biscuit mix and bake up a plate of Grandma's Peanut Butter Kisses. Whatever your sweet tooth, you'll find something here to satisfy you and your family and friends.

Stocking Your Pantry

Lazy cake recipes require very few ingredients. But in order to be prepared for baking on a whim, here are a few key items you'll want to have on your shelf, along with some common substitutions.

CAKE MIX

You'll find a wide variety of boxed cake mixes in the baking aisle of your local grocery store. Keep an eye out for deals—many stores offer discounts when you buy in bulk. Stock up on your favorite brands of vanilla, chocolate, and lemon cake mix.

BISCUIT MIX

Biscuit mix is a great base for baking cookie and cake recipes.

COOL WHIP

A tub of Cool Whip or a comparable brand of whipped topping is a key ingredient in many lazy cake recipes. Always keep some on hand so you can whip up a batch of cookies in no time.

COCONUT OIL

Coconut oil is a healthy and flavorful substitution for canola or olive oil. Coconut oil adds a delicious, tropical flavor to whatever you're baking and goes well with chocolate, lemon, and vanilla cake mix. Don't hesitate to include this in any of your recipes—especially those calling for shredded coconut.

PREMADE GRAHAM CRACKER PIE CRUSTS

Graham cracker crusts make a great crunchy base for many of the pies and desserts in this book. Buy them in the grocery store, or make your own ahead of time and store them in the freezer.

CREAM CHEESE

Cream cheese is such a versatile ingredient—use it in cakes, cookies, and pies.

OTHER COMMON INGREDIENTS

Vanilla

Eggs

Powdered sugar

Peanut butter

Sweetened condensed milk

Butter or margarine

Miniature marshmallows

Cream cheese

Semisweet chocolate chips (or white chocolate, extra-dark chocolate, or butterscotch chips)

Cinnamon

Healthy Substitutions

While cakes and cookies aren't exactly known for being healthy, we all need a bit of sweetness in our lives. With that said, there are lots of small changes you can make to these recipes to create healthier treats for you and your family.

For healthier fats: Recent studies have shown that the fats in butter are healthier for you than those in margarine. While many people switched from butter to margarine because margarine is lower in cholesterol, we now know that margarine is high in trans fat, which isn't good for us. I use butter in my recipes for that reason, but it's up to you. You can also try coconut oil instead of butter. Fellow bakers have recommended substituting half the amount of butter in a recipe for mashed avocado. Avocados are full of heart-healthy monounsaturated fatty acids.

For more antioxidants: Try using dark chocolate instead of milk chocolate. Look for chocolate that's 70 percent cocoa or higher. Using dark chocolate will make the recipe less sweet, so be forewarned.

For less sodium: Use unsalted butter to lower the sodium content of any recipe.

For less sugar: Try using half the amount of sugar and substituting apple-sauce for the rest.

Ethical eating: Many of us are trying to buy foods that are healthier not only for us but for the planet. If that's something you're interested in, look for labels that say organic, hormone-free, free-range, cage-free, or GMO-free. For example, many grocery stores now sell eggs that come from free-range chickens raised outdoors.

Equipment

Lazy cake recipes don't require any special baking equipment or fancy kitchen tools. In fact, many of these recipes don't even require an oven! But here are a few key things to have on hand before you get started.

- Stand mixer
- Hand mixer
- Whisk
- Measuring spoons
- Measuring cup
- Large mixing bowl
- Shallow bowl
- Muffin tins and mini muffin tins
- Cookie sheets
- Baking liners like parchment paper or silicone baking mats
- 9 x 13-inch pan

CHAPTER ONE

QUICK COOKIES

Lemon Dream Drops

These amazing lemon cookies have four ingredients and come together in seconds. You can omit the powdered sugar coating if you want, but the sugar adds a hint of sweetness to the gooey and tender interior.

Makes 3 dozen cookies

½ cup powdered sugar

1 egg

1 container (8 ounces) Cool Whip

1 box lemon cake mix

Preheat oven to 350°F. Pour powdered sugar into shallow bowl and set aside. Mix together the egg, Cool Whip, and cake mix until smooth. Batter will be thick. Roll cookie mixture into 1-inch balls. Place 2 inches apart on ungreased cookie sheets. Bake for 10 to 12 minutes. Directly after baking, gently roll cookies in powdered sugar to coat. Cool on wire racks.

Toasted Coconut
Macaroon Cookies

These light and toasted cookies make a tasty snack. Just roll the two ingredients together and pop them under the broiler. Enjoy your toasted coconut macaroons within minutes!

Makes 6 cookies

1 (14-ounce) can sweetened condensed milk

4 ounces (½ an 8-ounce package) unsweetened
shredded coconut

Preheat the broiler to medium. Pour ¾ of the can of condensed milk into a bowl and mix in the coconut until moist. Add more milk as necessary until desired consistency is reached. Shape the mixture into 6 balls and broil for 2 to 3 minutes or until golden brown.

Grandma's Peanut Butter Kisses

The texture of these cookies is nothing short of divine. You can even omit the chocolate kisses and they'll still be a big hit. They stay soft and delicious for up to a week in an airtight container.

Makes 3 dozen cookies

2 cups biscuit mix

¾ cup peanut butter

1 (14-ounce) can sweetened condensed milk

1 teaspoon vanilla

36 chocolate kisses, unwrapped

Preheat oven to 350°F. Mix together biscuit mix, peanut butter, condensed milk, and vanilla until smooth. Shape into 1-inch balls, and place 2 inches apart on ungreased cookie sheets. Bake for 8 to 10 minutes or until cookies start to turn golden brown. Directly after baking, press a chocolate kiss into center of each cookie. Cool on wire racks.

Oreo Cheesecake Cookies

Chunks of Oreo give a bit of crunch to these gooey cookies. Be sure to crush the cookies well, otherwise you'll have big chunks of cookie in your cheesecake—on second thought, maybe that's exactly what you want!

Makes 2 dozen cookies

1 (8-ounce) package cream cheese, softened

8 tablespoons butter, softened

¾ cup sugar

1 cup all-purpose flour

10 Oreo cookies, crushed

Beat together cream cheese and butter, then add sugar and beat well. Slowly add the flour and beat until incorporated. Fold in Oreos. Chill mixture for 1 hour. Preheat oven to 350°F. Scoop mixture in spoon-sized servings onto a lined cookie sheet. Bake cookies for 10 minutes.

Cinnamon Roll Cheesecake Cookies

These cookies are not only delicious, they will fill your kitchen with the comforting scent of sugar and cinnamon. In addition to its wonderful taste, cinnamon can regulate blood sugar, and smelling cinnamon can stimulate brain activity.

Makes 2 dozen cookies

1 (16.5-ounce) roll refrigerated sugar-cookie dough

1 box cheesecake-flavored pudding mix

1 cup white chocolate chips

1 teaspoon cinnamon

Preheat oven to 350°F. Combine all ingredients and mix well. Scoop in spoonfuls onto a lined baking sheet. Bake for 15 to 20 minutes or until golden brown.

Espresso Cookies

This grown-up treat combines brownie mix with coffee for an instant pick-me-up. Dust with a final sprinkling of instant coffee before serving for a slightly less sweet result.

Makes 2 dozen cookies

1 box brownie mix

2 tablespoons instant coffee, dissolved in 3 tablespoons hot water

1 egg

3 tablespoons oil

¼ teaspoon cinnamon

Preheat oven to 350°F. Mix all ingredients. Drop by spoonfuls onto a lined cookie sheet. Bake for 6 to 8 minutes.

Devil's Food
Cake Cookies

When chocolate is what you're craving, reach for these light cookies made with devil's food cake mix. While the name may be scandalous, the taste is pure heaven.

Makes 1 dozen cookies

1 box devil's food cake mix

½ cup vegetable oil

2 eggs

Preheat oven to 350°F. Blend cake mix, oil, and eggs until well combined. Drop by spoonfuls onto a lined cookie sheet and bake 10 to 12 minutes.

"Think what a better world it would be if we all, the whole world, had cookies and milk about three o'clock every afternoon and then lay down on our blankets for a nap."

—Barbara Jordan

Confetti Cake Cookies

These moist cookies make a great alternative to birthday cake. The cake-and-cookie combination is light tasting and can be easily adapted to any cake flavor.

Makes 1 dozen cookies

1 box confetti vanilla cake mix

1 teaspoon baking powder

2 eggs

⅓ cup vegetable oil

½ teaspoon vanilla

Preheat oven to 375°F. Mix together cake mix and baking powder. In a separate bowl, mix together eggs, oil, and vanilla. Add to the dry mixture and blend well. Spoon scoopfuls of mixture onto a lined baking sheet and bake for 8 to 10 minutes.

Chocolate Whoopie Pies

Everyone loves whoopie pies! These fun treats are made from chocolate cake mix and filled with sweet vanilla frosting. Feel free to swap out the vanilla for other frosting flavors depending on your preference.

Makes about 1 dozen whoopie pies

1 box chocolate cake mix

3 eggs

½ cup water

½ cup vegetable oil

1 (16-ounce) can vanilla frosting

Preheat oven to 400°F. Combine cake mix, eggs, water, and oil and blend well. Scoop batter into 1½-inch rounds and place on a lined baking sheet. Make sure you have an even number! Bake for 8 to 10 minutes and let cool. Cover flat side of one cookie with vanilla frosting and top with a second cookie (flat-side down). Repeat until all cookies have been made into whoopie pies.

Red Velvet Marshmallow Whoopie Pies

Marshmallow fluff and cream cheese make the light and tasty filling for these red velvet marshmallow whoopie pies. You can try different kinds of cake mix for different results, but this recipe is a solid classic to start with. Enjoy making whoopie pies!

Makes about 1 dozen whoopie pies

1 box red velvet cake mix

¼ cup butter, softened

2 eggs

1 (7-ounce) jar marshmallow fluff

4 ounces cream cheese, softened

Preheat oven to 350°F. Beat cake mix and butter until combined. Add eggs and blend well. Roll dough into 1-inch balls and place on a lined baking sheet. Bake for 7 to 9 minutes. Meanwhile, mix together fluff and cream cheese. When cookies are cool, frost flat side of one cookie with fluff mixture and top with a second cookie (flat-side down). Repeat with remainder.

CHAPTER TWO

LAZY CAKE BARS

Lazy Cake
Cookie Bars

This is a combination cake-and-cookie-bar. It's gooey and delicious and you can easily experiment with other flavors should you so desire—this recipe uses classic vanilla and chocolate. This is a great dessert to bring to a potluck or fundraiser.

Makes one 9 x 13-inch pan

1 box vanilla cake mix

2 eggs

1 stick butter, melted

2 cups chocolate chips

Preheat oven to 350°F. Grease a 9 x 13-inch pan with butter or cooking spray and set aside. Mix together all the ingredients until smooth. Spread in pan. Bake for 20 minutes or until golden brown. Cool in pan.

"My theory on housework is, if the item doesn't multiply, smell, catch fire, or block the refrigerator door, let it be. No one else cares. Why should you?"

—Erma Bombeck

Butterscotch-Spice Lazy Cake Cookie Bars

This is a delicious combination of butterscotch and spice. Let your sweet flag fly with this easy dessert treat.

Makes one 9 x 13-inch pan

1 box spice cake mix

2 eggs

1 stick butter, melted

2 cups butterscotch chips

Preheat oven to 350°F. Grease a 9 x 13-inch pan with butter or cooking spray and set aside. Mix together all the ingredients until smooth. Spread in pan. Bake for 20 minutes or until golden brown. Cool in pan.

Double-Chocolate Lazy Cake Cookie Bars

If you're like me and can't ever get enough chocolate, this is the recipe for you. Gooey chocolate chips nestled in warm chocolate cake make this the perfect treat for the chocoholics in your life. You can also use extra-dark chocolate chips for a less sweet version.

Makes one 9 x 13-inch pan

1 box chocolate cake mix

2 eggs

1 stick butter, melted

2 cups chocolate chips

Preheat oven to 350°F. Grease a 9 x 13-inch pan with butter or cooking spray and set aside. Mix together all ingredients until smooth. Spread in pan. Bake for 20 minutes or until firm to the touch. Cool in pan.

Chocolate contains theobromine, which is similar to caffeine. The compound is also found in some tranquilizers.

M&M's Lazy Cake Cookie Bars

Add a rainbow of color to your baking with these cookies made with real M&M's. These are great to make with the special-edition candies available seasonally—try green and red M&M's for a Christmasy treat, or use pastel M&M's for springtime or Easter baking.

Makes one 9 x 13-inch pan

1 box yellow cake mix
2 eggs
1 stick butter, melted
2 cups M&M's

Preheat oven to 350°F. Grease a 9 x 13-inch pan with butter or cooking spray and set aside. Mix together all the ingredients until smooth. Spread in pan. Bake for 20 minutes or until golden brown. Cool in pan.

Red Velvet Lazy Cake Cookie Bars

These red velvet cookie bars are a fun twist on a classic Southern dessert. The pecans add a satisfying crunch to these bars, but you can make them without nuts if you prefer.

Makes one 9 x 13-inch pan

1 box red velvet cake

2 eggs

1 stick butter, melted

2 cups white chocolate chips

1 cup chopped pecans

Preheat oven to 350°F. Grease a 9 x 13-inch pan with butter or cooking spray and set aside. Mix together all ingredients until smooth. Spread in pan. Bake for 20 minutes or until firm to the touch. Cool in pan.

Orange-Almond Lazy Cake Cookie Bars

The combination of orange and almonds is a classic one. These bars are great for a sweet option at brunch or a sophisticated alternative to brownies at potlucks and bake sales. The beautiful color of the orange cake and the subtle flavor of the nuts will make your tastebuds happy. No one will guess how easy they were to make.

Makes one 9 x 13-inch pan

1 box orange cake mix

2 eggs

1 stick butter, melted

½ cup chopped almonds

Preheat oven to 350°F. Grease a 9 x 13-inch pan with butter or cooking spray and set aside. Mix together all ingredients until smooth. Spread in pan. Bake for 20 minutes or until golden brown. Cool in pan.

Lemon Lazy Cake Cookie Bars

Whether you choose lemon or lime cake for this recipe, you'll be satisfied with these fresh-tasting citrus cookie bars. These make a nice springtime treat when you want something sweet but not too heavy.

Makes one 9 x 13-inch pan

1 box lemon or lime cake mix

2 eggs

1 stick butter, melted

½ cup lemon drops, crushed

Preheat oven to 350°F. Grease a 9 x 13-inch pan with butter or cooking spray and set aside. Mix together all ingredients until smooth. Spread in pan. Bake for 20 minutes or until golden brown. Cool in pan.

When life hands you lemons . . . make these cookie bars!

Peanut Butter Chocolate Lazy Cake Cookie Bars

Peanut butter and chocolate—what more can you ask for? This classic combination yields a satisfying treat. Enjoy them while they last, 'cause they won't last long!

Makes one 9 x 13-inch pan

1 box yellow cake mix

2 eggs

1 stick butter, melted

1 cup peanut butter chips

1 cup milk chocolate chips

Preheat oven to 350°F. Grease a 9 x 13-inch pan with butter or cooking spray and set aside. Mix together all the ingredients until smooth. Spread in pan. Bake for 20 minutes or until golden brown. Cool in pan.

Chocolate Toffee Lazy Cake Cookie Bars

Toffee is great for baking, as it melts easily and adds wonderful flavor and texture to any recipe. Made from sugar and butter, toffee works well with ingredients like chocolate, nuts, cream, or whiskey. In this recipe, chocolate cake and sweet toffee chips combine to create a sweet, gooey bar that your friends and family will love.

Makes one 9 x 13-inch pan

1 box chocolate cake mix

2 eggs

1 stick butter, melted

2 cups toffee chips

Preheat oven to 350°F. Grease a 9 x 13-inch pan with butter or cooking spray and set aside. Mix together all the ingredients until smooth. Spread in pan. Bake for 20 minutes or until firm to the touch. Cool in pan.

Peanut Butter Banana Spice Lazy Cake Cookie Bars

Elvis Presley loved his peanut butter and banana sandwiches—and with good reason. Peanut butter and banana tastes almost as good as peanut butter and jelly. You'll love this cookie bar made from peanut butter, banana, and spice cake mix.

Makes one 9 x 13-inch pan

1 stick butter, melted

¼ cup peanut butter

1 box spice cake mix

2 eggs

1 medium banana, mashed

Preheat oven to 350°F. Grease a 9 x 13-inch pan with butter or cooking spray and set aside. Stir together the butter and peanut butter until smooth. Add the rest of the ingredients and mix well. Spread in pan. Bake for 20 minutes or until golden brown. Cool in pan.

Mint Chocolate Lazy Cake Cookie Bars

If you love mint like I do, you'll be drawn to the recipes in this book featuring both mint and chocolate. This cookie bar recipe is great when you want something sweet but not too sweet.

Makes one 9 x 13-inch pan

1 box yellow cake mix

2 eggs

1 stick butter, melted

2 cups mint chocolate chips, or chopped chocolate mint candies

5 or 6 drops green food coloring, optional

Preheat oven to 350°F. Grease a 9 x 13-inch pan with butter or cooking spray and set aside. Mix together cake mix, eggs, butter, and chips until smooth. If using food coloring, fold it in a few drops at a time until the batter is the color you want. Spread in pan. Bake for 20 minutes or until firm to the touch. Cool in pan.

Lemon Bars

Simple. Fresh. Delicious. Lemons were brought to the Americas by Christopher Columbus and are now grown extensively in Florida and California. This recipe calls for lemon pie filling and angel food cake, which combine to make a light cookie bar. Don't forget to dust with powdered sugar before serving!

Makes one 9 x 13-inch pan

1 box angel food cake mix

1 can lemon pie filling

Powdered sugar, for sprinkling

Preheat oven to 350°F. Grease a 9 x 13-inch pan with butter or cooking spray and set aside. Mix cake mix and pie filling until moistened. Spread in pan. Bake for about 20 minutes. Cool in pan, then cut into bars and sprinkle with powdered sugar.

Peanut Butter Chocolate Squares

This is a simple no-bake recipe with great-tasting results. Smooth peanut butter will make the mixture easier to spread and cut, but feel free to use crunchy peanut butter if you're feeling adventurous.

Makes 3 dozen squares

1½ cups graham cracker crumbs

1 (1-pound) bag powdered sugar

1½ cups peanut butter

1 cup butter, melted

1 (12-ounce) bag chocolate chips

Combine the graham cracker crumbs, powdered sugar, and peanut butter and mix well. Add melted butter and blend well. Press mixture evenly into a 9 x 13-inch pan. Melt chocolate chips in microwave and spread over peanut butter mixture. Chill until set and cut into bars. (Don't chill too long or they will be difficult to cut.)

Cake Batter Cheesecake Bars

These cheesecake bars may be nontraditional, but they taste delicious. They also travel well, so pack some up for long car rides, parties, or a snack on the go. If you're so inclined, add some rainbow or chocolate sprinkles to the mix. Because everyone loves sprinkles!

Makes one 9 x 13-inch pan

3 (8-ounce) packages cream cheese, softened

1 (14-ounce) can sweetened condensed milk

2 tablespoons vanilla

3 eggs

1 box yellow cake mix

Preheat oven to 375°F. Lightly grease a 9 x 13-inch pan. Beat together the cream cheese, sweetened condensed milk, and vanilla until smooth. Beat in the eggs and slowly add the cake mix. Fold in the sprinkles, if using. Pour the batter into the pan and bake for 40 minutes. Chill for 4 hours before serving.

Almost-Homemade Cheesecake Bars

This variation on Cake Batter Cheesecake Bars (previous recipe) is a little more complicated, in that the cake layer forms a sort of crust on the bottom. This cooks at a lower temperature than you might be used to, but the result is outrageous.

Makes one 9 x 13-inch pan

CRUST

1 box yellow cake mix

1 egg

½ cup butter, melted

FILLING

1 (8-ounce) package cream cheese, softened

2 eggs

1 (16-ounce) box confectioner's sugar

Preheat oven to 300°F. Lightly grease a 9 x 13-inch pan. Beat together the cake mix, 1 egg, and the melted butter until a smooth dough forms. Pat dough into prepared pan. Wipe out bowl, and beat the cream cheese until fluffy, about a minute or two. Add the remaining 2 eggs, one at a time, beating until egg is incorporated completely. Add the confectioner's sugar slowly, about a cup at a time. This will be a very thick batter. Spread filling over cake layer. Bake for 40 to 50 minutes.

Coconutty
Nut Bars

Almost everyone has tried some variation of this cookie bar. You can add chocolate chips if you are so inclined. These bars are very, very sweet, so a little bite goes a long way. I'd suggest cutting them into 16 squares. Your dentist will thank you.

Makes one 9 x 9-inch square pan

CRUST

¼ cup butter, melted

1 cup graham cracker crumbs (or other cookie crumbs)

TOPPING

1 cup chopped mixed nuts

1 cup shredded coconut

1 (14-ounce) can sweetened condensed milk

1 (12-ounce) bag chocolate chips, optional

Preheat oven to 350°F. Grease a 9 x 9-inch square pan with butter or cooking spray. Mix together butter and cookie crumbs until well blended. Press into pan. Sprinkle chips, nuts, and coconut evenly over the top. Pour sweetened condensed milk over that. Bake for 30 minutes or until coconut starts to brown.

CHAPTER THREE

PIES AND PUDDINGS

Chocolate Hazelnut Pie

Chocolate hazelnut spread mixed with Cool Whip and cream cheese gives this no-bake pie a silky texture and a satisfyingly rich taste. Serve on a hot summer day or anytime you need a quick dessert with a "wow" factor.

Makes one 9-inch pie

1 (13-ounce) jar chocolate hazelnut spread, divided

1 (9-inch) prepared graham cracker pie crust

1 (8-ounce) package cream cheese, softened

1 (8-ounce) container Cool Whip, thawed

¼ cup crushed hazelnuts, optional

Spread ¼ cup of the hazelnut spread over the graham cracker crust. Beat remaining hazelnut spread and cream cheese together in a bowl until smooth. Fold Cool Whip into the cream cheese mixture. Spread evenly over the pie crust. Sprinkle with hazelnuts, if using. Refrigerate at least 4 hours and serve.

"There's nothing better than a good friend, except a good friend with chocolate."
—Linda Grayson

Lemon Ice-Box Pie

This lemon pie is light and refreshing—and doesn't require any baking. Whip one up in minutes and then pop it in your "ice box" until it's ready to serve! This looks especially appealing when served with a lemon-slice garnish.

Makes one 9-inch pie

1 (8-ounce) container of Cool Whip

1 (14-ounce) can of sweetened condensed milk

1 packet of lemonade mix (2-quart size)

1 premade graham cracker pie crust

Combine Cool Whip, condensed milk, and lemonade mix. Mix well until blended and thick. Spread evenly into pie crust. Refrigerate 4 to 6 hours.

S'mores Pies

These bring back memories of sitting around a campfire toasting marshmallows (although we made our fair share of s'mores in the microwave as well). These mini baked s'mores are great for parties and sleepovers, and they're a lot less messy than the campfire version.

Makes 6 mini pies

1 cup chocolate chips

1 package mini graham cracker pie crusts

1 cup marshmallows

Preheat oven to 375°F. Place a tablespoon of chocolate chips into each mini pie crust, then top with a layer of marshmallows. Bake for 10 minutes. Serve immediately.

Mini Cheesecakes

Is there anything better than cheesecake? If there is, it's mini cheesecake! These single-serving cakes are perfectly portioned for an easy dinner-party dessert and are great for wedding and baby showers. Top with your favorite berries or pie filling if you like.

Makes 4 dozen mini cheesecakes

1 package vanilla wafers

2 packages cream cheese, room temperature

¾ cup sugar

2 eggs

1 teaspoon vanilla

Preheat oven to 350°F. Line a mini muffin tin with liners. Place a vanilla wafer into the bottom of each muffin cup. Mix cream cheese with sugar, vanilla, and eggs. Fill each muffin cup halfway, and bake for 15 minutes.

Key Lime Pie

Key lime pie originated in the Florida Keys, where limes were plentiful and residents didn't feel much like baking in the heat. If you like your key lime pie with a bright pop of lime green, feel free to add food coloring; it will taste tangy and delicious either way. Serve topped with whipped cream and a slice of lime for a refreshing summery dessert.

Makes one 9-inch pie

1 (8-ounce) package cream cheese, softened

1 (8-ounce) can of sweetened condensed milk

½ cup of lime juice

1 prepared graham cracker crust

1 teaspoon green food coloring, optional

Put the softened cream cheese in a bowl and mix with a hand mixer until creamy. Add the condensed milk and mix until combined. Add the lime juice and the food coloring, if using. Mix until combined. Spread mixture evenly onto pie crust and refrigerate for 1 hour until set. Top with whipped cream or a slice of lime and serve.

Candy Pie

Butterfinger candies are some of my favorite treats. Created in 1923 by a Chicago businessman named Otto Schnering, Butterfinger benefited from a creative publicity stunt: to promote its new candy bars, Schnering's company dropped the chocolate confections from airplanes over major American cities. Now nearing its 100th birthday, Butterfinger is celebrated in this candy pie. Serve this pie with chocolate sauce if you're feeling decadent.

Makes one 9-inch pie

1 (8-ounce) package cream cheese, softened

1 (12-ounce) container Cool Whip

6 Butterfinger (or other variety) candy bars, crushed

1 premade graham cracker pie crust

1 pint vanilla ice cream, softened

Mix together cream cheese and Cool Whip until smooth. Fold in crushed candy until incorporated. Pour into crust. Carefully spread ice cream over top and freeze for at least 2 hours.

Tropical Sunshine Fluff

Fluff is made from combining Cool Whip with marshmallows and adding a bunch of other delicious ingredients. In this recipe we've used vanilla pudding mix, coconut, and crushed pineapple (including the juice). Serve with a rum cocktail and enjoy an extra tropical dessert!

Makes 1 large bowl

1 (3.4-ounce) package vanilla instant pudding mix

1 (20-ounce) can crushed pineapple, undrained

1 (8-ounce) container Cool Whip, thawed

2 cups miniature marshmallows

1 cup shredded coconut

Combine vanilla pudding mix and pineapple in a bowl. Fold in the rest of the ingredients. Chill for 1 hour before serving.

"I am starting to think that maybe memories are like dessert. I eat it, and it becomes a part of me, whether I remember it later or not."

—Erica Bauermeister

Cherry-Berry Fluff

Cherries are a wonderful dessert for the summer months or for those winter months when you need a sweet reminder of summer. This is a flavorful treat and can be served over graham crackers or pie crust as desired.

Makes 1 large bowl

1 (8-ounce) container Cool Whip, thawed

1 (14-ounce) can sweetened condensed milk

1 (21-ounce) can cherry pie filling

1 (20-ounce) can crushed pineapple, drained

2 cups miniature marshmallows

Shredded coconut (optional garnish)

Mix together all ingredients. Chill for 1 hour before serving. Add shredded coconut as a garnish.

Strawberry Cream Fluff

Strawberries and cream come together perfectly in this summery dessert. This recipe calls for frozen strawberries, so you can enjoy this treat year round. Top with fresh strawberries and whipped cream for a beautiful presentation.

Makes 1 large bowl

1 (10-ounce) bag frozen strawberries

1 (18-ounce) jar strawberry preserves

1 (14-ounce) can sweetened condensed milk

1 (16-ounce) container Cool Whip, thawed

Thaw the strawberries, then strain and mash them. Combine the mashed strawberries with the preserves and condensed milk. Fold in the Cool Whip until evenly combined. Chill for 1 hour before serving.

Black Forest
Mousse

This is an easy dessert to whip together for friends and family. Morello cherries work great here, but you can substitute dried cherries if you want.

Makes 1 large bowl

2 chocolate pudding snack cups

1½ cups Cool Whip, plus more for garnishing

1 (4-ounce) jar morello cherries, drained

½ cup dark chocolate chips

2 tablespoons cherry liquor, optional

Combine pudding and whipped topping. Fold in the cherries and the chocolate chips. Spoon into small bowls and garnish with chocolate chips and more Cool Whip.

Cherry Pie Cookie Cups

Sweet cherry pie filling gives these cookies a pop of color that looks great on the plate and tastes delicious!

Makes 2 dozen cookie cups

1 (16.5-ounce) roll refrigerated sugar-cookie dough

1 (21-ounce) can cherry pie filling

1 cup powdered sugar

1 tablespoon butter, melted

1–2 tablespoons milk

Preheat oven to 350°F. Line a mini muffin pan with liners. Divide cookie dough in half and cut each half into 12 pieces. Roll each piece into a ball and place in muffin cups. Bake for 15 minutes. Remove from oven and press down center of each cookie to make an indentation. Fill centers with a spoonful of cherry pie filling. Return to oven and bake an additional 3 to 5 minutes. Mix the powdered sugar, butter, and milk together and drizzle over cooled cookies.

No-Bake Chocolate Éclair Dessert

While we all love good French pastry, we seldom have the time or energy to create them. That's why I love this no-bake dessert that feels decadent but doesn't take a lot of time to make. Warmed fudge sauce poured over the top just before eating tastes great, but chocolate frosting will also do the trick.

Makes one 9 x 13-inch pan

1 (3.5-ounce) box vanilla instant pudding mix

2 cups milk

1 (8-ounce) container Cool Whip

Graham crackers

Chocolate frosting, chocolate fudge sauce, or cocoa powder

Beat the pudding mix and milk, then stir in the Cool Whip. Line bottom of pan with graham crackers and spread half the pudding mixture over the crackers. Add another layer of crackers and top that with rest of the pudding mixture. Top with a final layer of crackers. Top that with chocolate frosting or warmed chocolate fudge sauce.

Pear Tarts

Simple, flavorful, and elegant—nothing beats a scrumptious pear tart. You can use individual tart pans, or, if you don't have them, a muffin tin.

Makes 4 tarts

1 package refrigerated pastry dough

1 (15-ounce) can pear halves

½ cup apricot or peach jam

Preheat oven to 400°F. Line tart pans with pastry dough. Thinly slice the pears and arrange them in the pans so they overlap. Warm the jam in the microwave and pour over the pear slices. Bake for 30 to 35 minutes or until crust is golden brown and the filling bubbles.

"Dessert is to a meal what a dress is to a woman."

—Beatrice Peltre

CHAPTER FOUR

COOKIE BALLS

Chocolate Chip Cheesecake Balls

Cheesecake balls are seriously addictive. This is also a kid-friendly recipe, as little ones love to roll the balled-up dough in the pile of chocolate chips! Remember to refrigerate the mixture for at least an hour, otherwise the balls won't hold their shape.

Makes 1 dozen balls

½ cup butter, softened

1 (8-ounce) package cream cheese, softened

1 cup powdered sugar

1 teaspoon vanilla

2 cups mini chocolate chips, divided

Cream together the butter and cream cheese. Add the sugar and vanilla and beat well. Fold in half the chocolate chips. Refrigerate in bowl at least 1 hour. Spread remaining chips over waxed paper or a floured surface. Scoop out a spoonful of the cream cheese mixture, form into a ball with your fingers, and roll ball in chips until covered.

Butterscotch Chip
Cheesecake Balls

Butterscotch is such a great flavor to bake with. This recipe calls for mini butter-scotch chocolate chips, and their brown sugar and butter flavor is complemented by even more brown sugar and butter! Yum!

Makes 1 dozen balls

½ cup butter, softened

1 (8-ounce) package cream cheese, softened

1 cup powdered sugar

2 tablespoons brown sugar

2 cups mini butterscotch chips, divided

Cream together the butter and cream cheese. Add the powdered sugar and brown sugar and beat well. Fold in half the butterscotch chips. Refrigerate in bowl at least 1 hour. Spread remaining chips over waxed paper or a floured surface. Scoop out a spoonful of the cream cheese mixture, form into a ball with your fingers, and roll ball in chips until covered.

Peanut Butter Chip Cheesecake Balls

Did you know "peanut paste" was originally marketed as a dental aid in the late 1800s? Luckily for us, a man named C. H. Summer introduced peanut paste to the world at the 1904 World's Fair in St. Louis—and peanut butter as we know it today was born. These peanut butter balls are truly indulgent and go well with a tall glass of milk.

Makes 1 dozen balls

¼ cup peanut butter

1 (8-ounce) package cream cheese

2 cups powdered sugar

½ teaspoon vanilla

2 cups mini peanut butter chips, divided

Cream together the peanut butter and cream cheese. Add the sugar and vanilla and beat well. Fold in half the peanut butter chips. Refrigerate in bowl at least 1 hour. Spread remaining chips over waxed paper or a floured surface. Scoop out a spoonful of the cream cheese mixture, form into a ball with your fingers, and roll ball in chips until covered. For extra peanut flavor, add crushed peanuts to the peanut-butter-chip topping.

Mint Chocolate Chip Cheesecake Balls

Chocolate and mint are a classic flavor combination. This recipe calls for just a hint of mint, so the taste is subtle. Mint is a great digestive, making these a perfect after-dinner treat. You could add a splash of green food coloring to the mix if desired for an extra pop of color. Garnish with crushed mint leaves for a special presentation.

Makes 1 dozen balls

½ cup butter, softened

1 (8-ounce) package cream cheese, softened

1 cup powdered sugar

¾ teaspoon mint flavoring

2 cups mini chocolate chips, divided

Cream together butter and cream cheese. Add the powdered sugar and mint flavoring and beat well. Fold in half the chocolate chips. Refrigerate in bowl at least 1 hour. Spread remaining chips over waxed paper or a floured surface. Scoop out a spoonful of the cream cheese mixture, form into a ball with your fingers, and roll ball in chips until covered.

The ancient Romans believed that eating mint could increase your intelligence.

Decadent Dark-Chocolate Cheesecake Balls

These cheesecake balls made with dark chocolate chips and cocoa powder make for a rich-tasting romantic treat. Dark chocolate is thought to be an aphrodisiac and it's also a powerful antioxidant. Look for chocolate with more than 70 percent cocoa to get the most antioxidant benefits. Serve these with a dusting of cocoa powder or drizzle them with hot fudge sauce.

Makes 1 dozen balls

½ cup butter, softened

1 (8-ounce) package cream cheese, softened

¾ cup powdered sugar

¼ cup cocoa powder

2 cups mini dark chocolate chips, divided

Cream together butter and cream cheese. Add the sugar and cocoa powder and beat well. Fold in half the dark chocolate chips. Refrigerate in bowl at least 1 hour. Spread remaining chips over waxed paper or a floured surface. Scoop out a spoonful of the cream cheese mixture, form into a ball with your fingers, and roll ball in chips until covered.

Oreo Balls

This recipe makes Oreo cookies even more fun to eat! These cookie balls are great for birthday parties and holidays. For a yummy Halloween treat, keep an eye out for limited-edition orange-creme Oreos, in stores seasonally.

Makes 1 dozen balls

1 (16-ounce) package Oreo cookies, crushed

1 (8-ounce) package cream cheese, softened

1 (12-ounce) bag mini chocolate chips

Using a blender, mix the crushed Oreos and cream cheese together. Spread chocolate chips over waxed paper or a floured surface. Scoop out a spoonful of the mixture, form into a ball with your fingers, and roll ball in chips until covered.

Rum Balls

These rum balls are part crunchy wafer, part chocolate, and part fun! Use a dark spiced rum like Appleton or Captain Morgan for best results. Serve these adult-only treats alongside a rum punch if you're feeling indulgent.

Makes 2 dozen balls

1 cup chocolate chips

¼ cup light corn syrup

¾ cup dark rum

1 cup powdered sugar, and more for dusting

1 (12-ounce) box vanilla wafer cookies, crushed

Heat chocolate chips and corn syrup in a saucepan over low heat, stirring often, until chocolate is melted. Remove from heat and stir in rum and powdered sugar until dissolved. Fold in wafer crumbs. Refrigerate mixture for 15 to 20 minutes until dough is firm. Roll mixture into balls on waxed paper or a floured surface. Dust with powdered sugar and refrigerate before serving.

Peanut Butter Oatmeal Balls

Peanut butter and oatmeal is a flavor combination that reminds me of afternoons spent at my grandmother's house in Iowa. She loved to bake cookies and this combination was always a hit with the grandkids. This modern reimagining delivers all the great flavor of oatmeal and peanut butter in a fun "popable" form. Bet you can't eat just one!

Makes 2 dozen balls

1 cup peanut butter

¼ cup honey

1½ cups old-fashioned oats

½ cup mini chocolate chips

½ cup dried cranberries

Mix together peanut butter and honey until smooth. Add the oats, mini chocolate chips, and cranberries and stir until incorporated. Mixture will be thick. Refrigerate in bowl at least 1 hour, then roll into balls.

Coffee Cookie Balls

This rich coffee flavor of this recipe is rounded out by the sweet delicious taste of cookies! This is a caffeinated adult treat perfect for work events or autumn potlucks.

Makes 1 dozen balls

1 (8-ounce) package cream cheese, softened

2 tablespoons instant coffee, divided

1 (12-ounce) package vanilla wafer cookies, crushed

1 (7-ounce) container dipping chocolate

Mix together cream cheese, 1 tablespoon instant coffee, and cookie crumbs. Refrigerate in bowl at least 1 hour. Melt the dipping chocolate in the microwave according to directions. Stir in remaining instant coffee. Scoop out a spoonful of the cream cheese mixture, form into a ball with your fingers, and dip into chocolate. Let balls harden.

S'Mores Peanut Butter Balls

Whether you're sitting at the campfire telling spooky stories or lounging around the house watching cartoons with your kids, this is a tasty treat.

Makes 1 dozen balls

¾ cup peanut butter

¼ cup marshmallow cream

1 cup graham cracker crumbs

1 cup chocolate chips

1 (7-ounce) container dipping chocolate

Mix together peanut butter, marshmallow cream, graham cracker crumbs, and chocolate chips. Mixture will be thick. Refrigerate in bowl at least 1 hour. Melt the dipping chocolate in the microwave according to directions. Scoop out a spoonful of the cookie mixture, form into a ball with your fingers, and dip in chocolate. Let balls harden.

CHAPTER FIVE

CUPCAKES, MUFFINS, AND MORE

Cherry Coke Soda-Can Cupcakes

Cupcakes made with only a can of soda and a box of cake mix may sound too good to be true—but trust me these are easy and delicious. Soda-can cupcakes can be made with any flavor of cake mix and soda. So get creative and have fun!

Makes 1½ dozen cupcakes

1 box vanilla cake mix

1 can Cherry Coke, room temperature

1 (16-ounce) container vanilla frosting

Preheat oven to 350°F. Line a muffin pan with liners. Combine soda and cake mix and beat on low for 3 minutes. Fill muffin cups three-quarters full with batter. Bake for 18 to 20 minutes or until toothpick inserted in center comes out clean. Cool and top with vanilla frosting.

"I've never met a problem a proper cupcake couldn't fix." —Sarah Ockler

Dr. Pepper Soda-Can Cupcakes

Red velvet cake and Dr. Pepper make for a great soda-cake combination with classic southern flavors. What other flavor combinations can you think of? The possibilities are endless, but a good rule of thumb for beginners is to use fruit-flavored sodas like grape or orange and a vanilla cake base.

Makes 1½ dozen cupcakes

1 box red velvet cake mix

1 can Dr. Pepper, room temperature

1 (16-ounce) container vanilla frosting

Preheat oven to 350°F. Line a muffin pan with liners. Combine cake mix and soda and beat on low for 3 minutes. Fill muffin cups three-quarters full with batter. Bake for 18 to 20 minutes or until toothpick inserted in center comes out clean. Cool and top with vanilla frosting.

Pumpkin Spice Muffins

There are so many delicious ways to use that can of pumpkin puree that's been sitting in your pantry. This is one of my favorite recipes. The spice cake mix provides all the flavor you need. Top with some buttercream frosting to turn these snacks into a sweet dessert!

Makes 1 dozen muffins

1 box spice cake mix

1 (15-ounce) can pumpkin puree

Preheat oven to 400°F. Line a muffin pan with liners. Combine cake mix and pumpkin in a bowl and mix well. (The batter will be thick; resist the urge to add any liquid.) Fill muffin cups three-quarters full with batter. Bake for 18 to 20 minutes.

Chocolate Chip Apple-Pumpkin Muffins

The applesauce in these muffins makes them extra-moist, and if you use chunky applesauce, you'll have nice bits of apple as well. I love the flavor combination of pumpkin and chocolate, although you could use butterscotch chips for a sweeter taste.

Makes 1 dozen muffins

1 box vanilla cake mix

1 (15-ounce) can pumpkin puree

½ cup chunky applesauce

1 cup chocolate chips

Preheat oven to 350°F. Line a muffin pan with liners. Combine all ingredients and mix well. (The batter will be thick; resist the urge to add any liquid.) Fill muffin cups three-quarters full with batter. Bake for 18 to 20 minutes.

Apple Muffins

Easy apple muffins made with apple pie filling and vanilla cake mix are sure to impress. Make them in the autumn when the weather is cooler and you're looking for a delicious seasonal snack for the whole family.

Makes 1 dozen muffins

1 (18.25-ounce) package white cake mix

2 teaspoons apple pie spice

3 eggs

1 (21-ounce) can apple pie filling

Preheat oven to 350°F. Line a muffin pan with liners. Combine cake mix, apple pie spice, and eggs and mix well. Add apple pie filling and mix until just combined. Spoon batter into muffin cups and bake for 25 to 30 minutes.

An apple a day keeps the doctor away.

Cinnamon Cream Cheese Rolls

This variation on traditional cinnamon buns is not only delicious but fun to make. Kids love rolling up the bread and dipping it into the melted butter and cinnamon-and-sugar concoction. This flaky dessert is a great snack food at parties and also makes for an indulgent breakfast treat.

Makes 24 rolls

6 slices white bread

1 (4-ounce) package cream cheese, softened

1 tablespoon cinnamon

¾ cup sugar

½ cup butter, melted

Preheat oven to 350°F. Cut the crusts from the bread and flatten bread with a rolling pin. Spread the cream cheese over each piece of bread and roll tightly. Slice each one into 4 "rolls." Mix the cinnamon and sugar together and set aside in a shallow bowl. Dip the top of the rolls in the melted butter and then roll in the cinnamon-and-sugar mixture. Place on a lined baking sheet and bake for 20 minutes or until browned.

Piña Colada Cake

If you like pina coladas . . . *this recipe is for you. Pineapple and shredded coconut are a perfect, tropical combination. Can't you just hear the sound of the waves crashing against the beach? Serve slices topped with a little paper umbrella for a fun party decoration.*

Makes one 9 x 13-inch cake

1 box angel food cake mix

1 (20-ounce) can crushed pineapple, undrained

1 cup shredded coconut, divided

1 (8-ounce) container Cool Whip

Preheat oven to 350°F. Grease a 9 x 13-inch pan with butter or cooking spray. Combine cake mix and pineapple, including juices. Mix well. Pour into prepared pan and bake for 30 to 40 minutes until golden brown. Cool completely and sprinkle with half the coconut. Top with Cool Whip and sprinkle with remaining coconut to garnish.

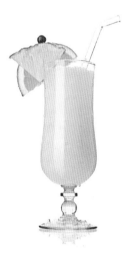

Pineapple Rum Cake

Tropical island flavors come together in this adults-only rum and pineapple cake. Serve this up and watch the party come to life!

Makes 1 tube cake

1 box angel food cake mix

1 (20-ounce) can crushed pineapple, undrained

½ cup butter

1 cup brown sugar

½ cup dark rum

Preheat oven to 350°F. Grease a tube pan with butter. Combine cake mix and pineapple with juices and mix well. Pour batter into tube pan. Bake for 40 minutes. Let cool and remove from pan. Melt butter and mix in brown sugar until dissolved, then add rum. Prick cake all over with a fork and pour rum glaze over top.

Hawaiian Banana Bread

Macadamia nuts, bananas, and coconut are combined here with simple yellow cake mix to create a delicious, moist banana bread that's a bit out of the ordinary. You can add more or less macadamia nuts or coconut depending on your taste and how crunchy you like your bread.

Makes 2 loaves

1 box yellow cake mix

⅓ cup oil

3 eggs

1½ cups banana, mashed

1 cup chopped macadamia nuts

1 cup shredded coconut, optional

Preheat oven to 350°F. Grease 2 loaf pans with butter or cooking spray. Beat cake mix, oil, eggs, and banana together until smooth, then add the nuts and coconut if using. Pour mixture into loaf pans and bake for 45 to 50 minutes.

Chocolate Cookie Log Roll

This chocolate cookie log roll is great for holiday parties. It's basically a train of sandwich cookies that goes on and on. The cookies soften overnight and become almost like a cake. For a less decadent treat, omit the final coating of Cool Whip and sprinkles.

Makes 1 log

1 (8-ounce) container Cool Whip, divided

1 package round chocolate wafers

1 tablespoon chocolate sprinkles

Using about half of the Cool Whip and reserving the rest, spread about a teaspoon of Cool Whip on a chocolate wafer and top with another wafer. Spread Cool Whip on top of that wafer and repeat. Lay the sandwiched cookies lengthwise on a plate and continue adding wafers and Cool Whip until you don't have any more cookies. Wrap the cookie log in aluminum foil and refrigerate overnight. Remove foil and top with the remaining Cool Whip and chocolate sprinkles before serving.

Acknowledgments

Many thanks to Ann Treistman, Sarah Bennett, Devorah Backman, and Felicia Czochanski at The Countryman Press, and to everyone at W. W. Norton & Company. Thanks also to Andrea Young, who helped me perfect some of these recipes.

Index